MW00977864

An
Ethics primer
for children

Go Honest

Honesty   Kindness   Respect

by Anna Makris Sioles

1987© by Anna M. Sioles
Revised Editions 1996©, 2002©

ISBN: 0-9620893-0-3

Preface

This book is intended to serve as an ethical primer for children — to nurture honesty, kindness and respect. The thought-provoking situations are to be used as a basis for discussion between parent and child or teacher and student. — The inherent beauty and workability of this book is that it will enable the parent or teacher to impart his or her own philosophical wisdom to the child according to each situation presented.

The ideals of honesty, kindness and respect are everlasting. They have passed the test of time. Let us incorporate them into our lives to improve the societal quality of today. These ideals are fundamental to the survival of the universe and the dignity of man.

Suggested Uses for Primer

Be creative. Each page should elicit a discussion between adult and child. Encourage child or children to respond to and evaluate the moral that each illustration represents. Use the lead statements and/or questions on each page. Be sensitive and imaginative so that further questions will surface. Difficult words or concepts should be explained.

The adult can set examples of these virtues. PRAISE the children when they exhibit these high moral standards. Make lists of how and when to be kind, honest and respectful. Each day situations will appear that will lend themselves to the teaching of these values — USE THEM.

Each page should foster critical thinking and support for our traditional ethical standards. The likely development of a close bond between child and adult would be a wonderful bonus.

Table of Contents

Honesty

Tell the truth • Honesty counts • Return the change
Honesty is the best policy • Truth is always best
Accept responsibility • Lying is a bad habit
Truth is a good habit • Don't steal

Kindness

It's kind to share • Be kind to your elders • Kind to others
Don't gossip • Thoughtfulness • New boy in town
Try not to be jealous • Kindness • Say nice things
Don't taunt animals • How can you help

Respect

Accept differences • Let's compromise • Older people
Helping older people • Be considerate • Respect rights
Respect all animals • Don't be a bully • Respect property
Like yourself

Honesty

Chapter 1

George Washington

1. Sometimes it's hard to tell the truth because you'll get yelled at, but it doesn't feel good to lie.

2. How do you begin to feel every time you tell the truth?

3. Would you like your friend, family, teacher and classmates to tell the truth? Why?

Tell the Truth

1. If you got 100% by cheating, how would you feel?

2. When you earn a good grade on your own, it feels good. Why?

Honesty counts

What is honesty?
What is cheating?
Why shouldn't we cheat?
Why should we do our own work?

1. If you were the treasurer of a club and you collected a lot of money, why couldn't you keep it?

2. What would you do if the store clerk gave you too much change?

Return the change.

Is it always easy to be honest?
Why shouldn't we keep the change?

15

1. If you lose something, what kind of a person would you hope finds it? Why?

Honesty.

I can not keep it.

It's not my bicycle.

Would I like someone to keep something I lost?

1. What if no one is looking? Would you keep the money?

2. What if there is no reward? Should you still return it? Why?

3. What if you found a watch? What would you do?

Be honest.

How would you feel if you lost something?
You should try to return things you find.

1. You're in a candy store and no one is looking. Should you take some candy? Why?

2. If no one is watching at the theatre, should you sneak in? Why?

SUBWAY

Honesty.

Honesty is the best policy.
When you are honest you feel
happy about yourself.
What is a sneaky person?
An honest person can be trusted!
It's easy to do the right thing and be honest.
Try it and see. YOU WILL FEEL SO GOOD INSIDE.

1. What responsibilities do you have if you own a pet?

Tell the truth.

Sometimes we forget to do the right thing. It's all right to tell the truth and correct our mistake..

1. What should you do if you break the teacher's flower pot and she doesn't know who did it?

Tell the truth.

Accept responsibility for what you do.
Don't let others accept the blame for you.

1. What should you do on public
   transportation if they think you're
   underage and you're not? DO THE
   RIGHT THING. TELL THE TRUTH.

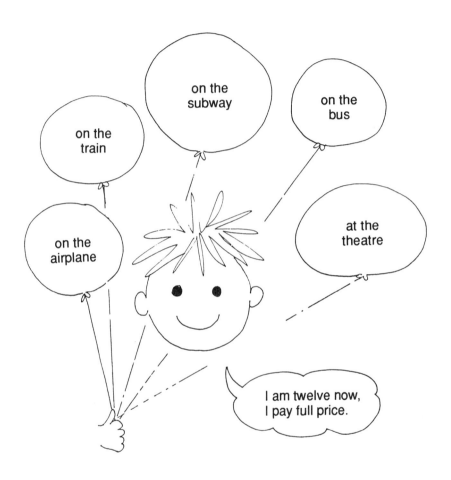

Doing the right thing is a good habit.

Lying is a bad habit.
Why?

1. What should you tell your father if you forgot to mail his important letter? Why is it difficult to tell the truth sometimes?

2. **Explain and discuss** - is there ever a time when telling the truth might hurt someone's feelings?

The truth is always best.

Being honest becomes a good habit.
Is it difficult to tell the truth
when someone is angry?

1. What is bad character?
   People who do not know right from
   wrong.

2. If you are older, smarter or stronger is it
   okay to take advantage of weaker people
   ... to take whatever you want? Why not?

3. Should he cheat his sister?

Be Honest!

Don't steal from others
It's WRONG! Get It!
DON'T STEAL!

1. Is it tempting to take money?
   Why shouldn't we?

2. What is a good way to record money given
   to you in trust?

3. It is an honor to collect money in TRUST.
   Your peers trust you. Don't let them down!
   EXERCISE your GOOD CONSCIENCE.

4. You will feel so good about yourself. YOU
   UPHELD THE HONOR SYSTEM. YOU
   TRIUMPHED OVER TEMPTATION. BE
   PROUD! YOUR SELF ESTEEM SOARS!

Don't Steal!!
They TRUST you.

HOW GOOD IT FEELS TO BE KIND!!

Kindness

Chapter 2

1. What would you do if your friend forgot his snack?

2. How do you feel when you share?

It's kind to share.

What kind things have you done?
What kind things can you do?

1. What could you do if the student next to you forgot his pencil or book?

2. **EXPLAIN** the dangers of sharing with strangers we don't know.

Be considerate.
How do friends help each other?

1. What things can we share with the homeless and needy people?

2. What would you do if one of your friends didn't share? What could you tell him?

Sharing.

What other things can we share?

1. What can you do to help all the lonely older people in nursing homes, etc.?

2. Discuss agencies you can contact for suggestions and procedures.

Be kind to your elders.

Why do some older people need help?
How do they feel?
Do you have any elderly relatives?
What are they like?

1. If Grandma or Grandpa are all alone now, what can you do for them?

2. What does it feel like to be alone, older and feel helpless? Try and think about it.

Thinking of others.

When you're kind to others,
the whole world is brighter!
How do people feel when you are kind to them?
How do you feel when you make others happy?

1. Would you like other people to say unkind things about you? Has this ever happened to you? How did you feel?

2. What nice things can we say about our friends, siblings, classmates, etc.? IF YOU CAN'T SAY NICE THINGS ABOUT OTHERS DON'T SAY ANYTHING.

Don't gossip. Gossip hurts.

Why does gossip hurt other people?
Does gossip hurt you?

1. How could we be more thoughtful at home with our family, or in school with our classmates?

Thoughtfulness

Why should we be thoughtful?
How does it feel to be sick and alone?

1. What could we do if a girl or boy doesn't know anyone and is eating lunch all alone?

2. What could we do if the new student has no one to share recess with?

A new boy in town is lonely.

How does the new boy feel?
What can we do to help him?
Does he or she come from another country?
Let us make them feel welcome.

1. If your friend got a high mark on a test in school or a new dog, should you be jealous? What might you do or say?

Try not to be jealous.

Be happy for others.
How does it feel to be jealous?
Why are we sometimes jealous?

TRY IN HOME AND CLASSROOM

1. If you train yourself to be kind, will it set a good example for others?

2. Try this in your family and classroom and see what happens. WHAT A NICE PLACE THE WORLD WOULD BE!

Kindness.

Love is everywhere when you are kind.
How do you feel when you make others happy?
How does it feel when you are happy
and love someone or something?

1. What will happen if you start to say nice things and act happy? Will it become a good habit?

2. What happens in a room when people say nice things to each other instead of hateful and angry words?

Say nice things about others if you can.

How do other people react when you
say nice things to them?
Do they feel pleased and happy?

1. What kind of world would we have without animals?

2. If we are kind to animals, how do they react?

Don't taunt animals.

Be kind — admire them.

Respect

Chapter 3

Respect the environment — it will take care of you.

Respect the rights of others.

Respect the opinions of others even though they may be different from yours.

Respect yourself. If you believe in yourself, so will others.

Respect the animals — they are wondrous and amazing.

1. How would you make the new student feel comfortable?

2. If a boy or girl has funny teeth, does it really matter? Can the person help it? Does it make the person bad?

Respect others.

We may look different, but we have
many of the same feelings.
What are some of those feelings?

1. If at playtime you want to play your favorite game and your friend wants to play a different one, what might you do?

2. What might you do if your brother and you both want to sit in the front of the car? ... if you each want to see a different movie? ... if you both want the same cookie and there is only one left?

Listen to and respect
the opinions of others
even though they are
different from yours.

Let's compromise.

What does compromise mean?
Should we always compromise?
Why not?

1. Why should we include older people in our conversations?

2. If Grandma were at the dinner table, how could we include her in our dinner conversation?

3. What are some of the things we learn from our elders?

4. If Grandpa wants to show you how to make a wooden boat, should you take the time to listen and learn? Why?

Older people are interesting.

What makes older people we know interesting?
Do you like to listen to your grandparents'
stories?

Helping older people.

Be considerate.

Respect elders.

In what other ways can we help older people?

1. What may happen if you bother an animal when it is eating or sleeping?

2. Do animals have the right to eat and sleep in peace?

3. Do your pets have fresh water and exercise too? DISCUSS the dangers of stray animals. It is best to call an adult when an animal is in danger.

Be considerate.

Respect their rights.

1. Why should we observe animals?

2. What can we learn from them?

3. Why should we respect them?

4. How do they help our environment?

Respect all animals.

They are wondrous and amazing.
Why are animals special?
What can they do?
Why are they important to our environment?

1. If you wake up early and you want to do something noisy, what should you do?

2. What if it's Mother's Day and your neighbor has pretty flowers? Would you cut them? Why not?

Respect the rights of others.

Why should we be nice to or neighbors?
What rights does a neighbor have?

1. If a young child has something you'd like, do you take it because you are bigger and stronger? Why not?

2. If you're on a lunch line in school, do you push ahead because you are bigger and stronger?

3. If you're at a birthday party, do you grab things first because you're bigger and stronger? Why not?

Don't be a bully.

What is a bully?
Why does he or she act that way?

1. If you break your neighbor's wagon, what might you do?

2. If you see your friends writing on a building, should you join them? Is that "cool?"

3. Why shouldn't you throw snowballs at cars?

Respect your environment.

Respect property.
How do you feel when someone
destroys something that is yours?

1. If you're at a park and see an injured bird, whom should you tell to call for help?

2. If your friends are carving a tree for fun, should you join them?

3. If you're at a class picnic and you are finished with your lunch, what do you do with your rubbish if there is no garbage can?

Don't destroy.

Respect property.
Why should we take care of our things?
Why should we take care of our environment?

1. What should you do if you borrow something from someone? How do you care for it?

2. If you borrowed a video from a friend and ruined it, what should you do? How?

Respect the property of others.

How do we like other people
to treat our things?

Don't Trust Everyone

You want to be nice
    and Honest
    and Kind
    and Respectful
but sometimes there
    are people that are
    not good
You must THINK!!
Keep away from people that
can harm you.

1. If you can remember all the times you did something virtuous, how does that make you feel?

2. If you're a nice person, shouldn't that make you feel PROUD, TERRIFIC, GREAT, CONFIDENT, SOooo HAPPY! and even "COOL?" TRY IT!!!

Respect yourself.

Like yourself.
How do you feel
when you do the right thing?